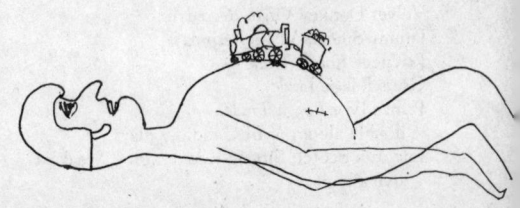

Works Extant

poetry

Large et Puffy	*Arc Publications*
Fresh Carpet	*Arc Publications*

prose

Gruts *(Methuen)* ill. Martin Honeysett
Life in a Scotch Sitting Room, vol. 2
    (Methuen) ill. Martin Honeysett
Fremsley *(Methuen)* ill. Martin Honeysett
Glasgow Dreamer *(Methuen)* ill. Martin Honeysett

children's books

Meal One *Heinemann* ill. Helen Oxenbury hb
Meal One *Armada Lions* ill. Helen Oxenbury pb
The Animal House *(Heinemann)*
    ill. Helen Oxenbury hb
The Animal House *Armada Lions*
    ill. Helen Oxenbury pb

albums

Dandruff *Virgin Records*
Velvet Donkey *Virgin Records*
Jammy Smears *Virgin Records*
Privilege *Rough Trade*
Gruts *Rough Trade*
Prince Ivor *Rough Trade*
    double album of BBC radio 3 plays
Life in a Scotch Sitting Room, vol. 2 *Speakout*
    live album

PRIVATE HABITS

by
Ivor Cutler
illustrated by
the author

Arc Publications

Published by Arc Publications
Nanholme Mill, Shaw Wood Road,
Todmorden, Lancs, OL14 6DA

Reprinted 1983, 1985, 1988, 1991.

Cover photos by David Campbell

Typeset by Bryan Williamson,
Manchester
Printed by Arc & Throstle Press Ltd,
Nanholme Mill, Todmorden, Lancs

ISBN 0 902771 89 2 paperback
ISBN 0 902771 90 6 hardback

Acknowledgements are due to *Ambit*,
BBC, *Doors*, *New Departures*, *New Poetry*,
Poetry Review and *Virgin Records*.

CONTENTS

THE HEAD OF A NAIL

The head of a nail is irregular. So is the point — and the shank. That is all there is to a nail.

Nails are dull.

A VARNISHED COATHOOK

A varnished coathook, embedded on a closet wall, drew my eye. It was warm, and upside down in the close summer air. On the door a hitherto cryptic notice — 'BALLOONS'.

THE BLONDE MOUSE

The blonde mouse curved her neck shyly at the compliment, letting the cheese hang limply on her claw. The eyes of the other females went hard and bright, and they determined to keep an eye on her, for she had an exasperating gait, a ripple across the haunches, that held the males in thrall.

CLEAR LIQUOR

The mouse lies by the river bank and looks placidly on to the water. He ignores the insects skating about, the drowning leaves. 'Look at the clear liquor!' he murmurs and tips his eye to the sky in amazement, terrified and cooled by the shadow of a newspaper blown from the face of a sleeping fisherman. As it settles over his frantic body, he eyes, 'from our political correspondent in Westminster.'

A PRAGMATIST

A small mouse beckons a large hornet. 'Teach me to fly.' Earnestly, he listens to a boring tale on instinctive technique, then, a pragmatist, launches into the air, to be punched to the ground by a bat. '…and keep your place, buster!'

AN ANCIENT TAMARISK

'I think I have broken something',
wheezed the mouse, kicking off her
corsets after a feverish day at the
fields. Her old spouse, no less weary,
put his slice of Cheshire to one side,
and, reaching out a wise claw, felt
around her ligaments for a swelling.
'Negative, my little ear of corn,' he
murmured through his cheese, and
lay back, to listen to the thin wind
disturbing light chaff, and the farther
sound of a brazen hoot from an ancient
tamarisk.

POTATO TUNE

A horse munches a field. Early evening fetches out singing potatoes. Carrots listen, revolving in their living quarters. I push a wicketkeeper's glove into the horizon, catch the sun, hold the day, hear potato tune for ever.

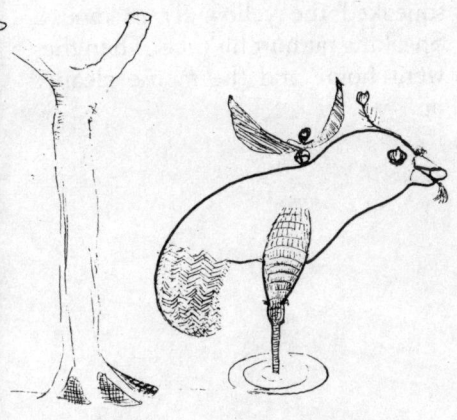

REALLY CHEWY

A mouse asked a rat and a yellow fly to
dine. The latter brought his friend, a
red fly. 'Is it all right? Will there be
enough?' he hummed. The mouse
produced a Gouda and they waded in.
'Delicious!' buzzed the rat, who spoke
fly with an accent. 'Really chewy!'
squeaked the yellow fly in mouse.
Speaking rat hurt his tube. Then they
went home and the mouse cleaned
up.

A MOUSE AND A TARANTULA

A mouse and a tarantula looked at one another with astonishment in a clearing. 'Six legs!' they murmured, quite incorrectly, and hurried off, shaking their little alive heads. All the flies burst out laughing, and went around pointing at one another and buzzing, '6 legs!' for the rest of the morning. One furry fly found a tiny piece of black tarantula dung.

BIG NED AND WEE BOB

Big Ned and Wee Bob travelled in a
row. Here, said Big Ned. So they sat.
After that they got up and looked in
their pocket mirrors. O.K. Let's go,
said Big Ned. O.K. said Wee Bob.

PRIVATE HABITS

I have private habits. So has everybody. What a relief! They are neither good, nor bad. I enjoy having them. They are much the same as yours. Notwithstanding, they will remain private, unless I am tortured by sadists consumed with curiosity.

RISOTTO

A climber is trapped on the shelf below, and, on the shelf below that are china plates, and, below that, dangling from hooks, are cups with handles and a milk jug. Granny scrapes risotto from last night into the sink. The climber will die because Granny knows he is not there. I shall not die because I am needed to unblock the risotto from the U-bend.

THE KEEPER

The keeper overwound the small birds so they live too quickly. Their tight jet eyes beg to be slowed, to be given time to consider. Consider, with a brain the size of a halibut liver oil capsule. No hands. No holidays. Just being alive and following your nature.

A MAN RETURNS

A man returns. His ladder lies on the wall. Daringly, for he is conventional, he mounts the rungs in the dark, but stops, to peer at the bricks, as though he had climbed a lady's legs out of curiosity. Suddenly empty, he descends and walks in striped trousers and black shoes to the door.

WINTER CIDER

He made winter cider from any small
fruit — scrabbling in the frost at
dawn — prying frozen twigs apart to
reach a coloured berry. Turning the
mangle uselessly in the washhouse
and pushing the little fellows through
loose rollers. Creaks were heard by all
in bed. Contented grins of 'winter
cider' from under the duvet. Frantic,
breath hanging from his lip in a loose
cloud: turn — turn — clank. Little
hard fruit balls fall again and again
into the enamel jug. At last he returns
with his empty burden, lays it on the
prepared breakfast table and sits for
hours on the corner chair waiting our
ecstatic surprise, tasting his winter
cider out our empty teacups, smacking
our cracked morning lips for his plea-

sure. He struts out the kitchen, eyes afire, narrow shoulders back, like a chicken, to his own breakfast of mash and water in the outhouse and a bite of stolen celery from under the straw. We drink coffee, read letters and brush crumbs off our gowns.

HAPPY HEN

The happiness of birds is not reflected on their faces. Strictly, birds do not have a face — just organs around the head. If a hen looks badtempered, it is due to a superficial disposal of its features, and if you place your ear by its beak, it may well be heard humming a contemporary dance tune in a happy, thready fashion.

THE OLD LADY DANCED

The old lady danced an assisted high-land fling for charity.

IF YOUR BREASTS

If your breasts are too big you will fall over, unless you wear a rucksack.

STONED DATES

A huge load of stoned dates sticks to the dock. Afraid of rain, wholesalers help stevedores. Soft brown insects gather and gossip as they pad over the mass.

A BLACK SNAKE

A black snake writhes along the river
bottom. Old plants watch. Vigorous
fry circle long puddles, prey to juicy
birds. Two crabs pinch a sparrow who
fell in and snapped a pale ankle.
Tumbleweed thunders along — grey
ballbearings — off to the sea for a
holiday. A black snake spies the damp
hole where a vole lived and curls in,
leaving two moonstones to guard.
Dark falls. Only fish sleep. The crabs
lean back, burp and pick their teeth.

I BUILT A ROAD

I built a road which had no purpose.
People gathered. "Where is it from?"
"Where does it go?" Then — "Is it a
road?" and — "What is it?" Specu-
lative builders narrowed their eyes.
Children crossed, stopped in the middle
and laughed. I have built a hut at
either end. One 'A', the other 'B'.
Sometimes I go from 'A' to 'B'. It
gives the road a bit of purpose — not
much.

A SHY LARK

Did you hear the lark? No. I saw him on the sky. It was so empty I joined him but he was shy and drifted off, so I sit on the grass. It is flat now, but will rise when I go. We do not praise grass enough. There goes the lark, pursued by a deaf hawk. What a menacing shadow it makes. A lark should carry a revolver.

BIG ENOUGH

'What a small barn!'

'Our harvest is small. Three blades of grass. We have no need for more. One blade, carefully consumed, lasts four months. Feel me! Good striped muscle. We lie in the sun and suck in health. See how I jump. Every night I count my fingers for diversion and watch the shadow on the wall. Our barn is big enough.'

THAT COAT

Where did you buy that coat? A little shop in Bond Street. It hangs a bit, but I walk to one side. Put your hand across the material. Can you feel the weave? When the threads cross like that, you know you've got a coat. The buttons are large. This coat was made for a tall woman so I altered the hem and adjusted the lining. See! It's tucked into the material throughout. I expect the lining's silk. The threads are rough and pick up fluff, but the colour is natural and sets off my dress below. I'm feeling good today. Paul will pick me up at six to go to Sadler's Wells. Goodness! I'll have to run. Give my love to Ben.

HEAVE HO

"Heave ho!" spoke a sailor. I jumped, as a packing case slipped past my shoulder into the sea. Thick bubbles from stowaways' lips inside burst with difficulty through the greasy surface scum as it sank, leaving me pensive. Their dignified silence. It could have been a crate of sherbet. "I like to see them go like that," boomed the captain in my ear. What he really said was, 'Why don't you love me? My clean body in its fresh white underwear.'

KNICKERS

I bought a pair of knickers but they did not feel comfortable and were chilly so I gave them to a woman.

No wonder they are cheaper than pants.

IN THE PARK

Whom did you see in the park? A big man in a dark suit. Was he by a tree? I saw him lean on the bark. He was trying to read a card but a wind twitched it and it fell. Eat this bread. It will make you tall. Here is hot tea too. Now. Watch this box while I work.

DO THAT AGAIN

Ever since I had wings and landed on
the table and everybody spilled their
soup and jumped up and shouted, I've
been happy. Do that again, said Dad.
So I did it. Then they finished their
soup and talked about what had happened. I landed on the ceiling and the
wall. I hovered for as much as a minute. I even stridulated, then hopped
across the room. It was easy to see I
had become a favourite. Yet, when
they went to bed, I was out the front
door. And stay there, you sneaky little
thing, called my erstwhile loving sister.
Still, there were spiders in the corners
and a good old moth with a musty
smell.

DRUM SKIN

In the sun a dove lands on a drum's skin to listen. The drummer slowly turns the drum till the creature's beak faces the afternoon. They both dream of other matters. Their smiles are reflected in a shaving mirror propped outside a wide tent.

A soldier's trumpet sends her to a tree.

LADIES' PLAITS

It has been asserted recently that ladies put their hair into buns to try to get men to realise that they too were sapient, the bun being an overflow skull for a superabundant brain. Men invariably accepted the bun as a silly ornament, unable to follow the reasoning, and the bun fell into desuetude. Now, some scientists are trying to correlate ladies' plaits with DNA, but they have their work cut out.

CHEAP CHOCOLATE

"I want privacy!" bellowed the huge man, full of water as a melon. We tiptoed out to the field at the end of the road and stood among the fragrant grasses, enjoying our fear, discussing his cogent need. At midnight we trouped back to discover him asleep on a bench, his buttons undone, a bar of cheap chocolate open in his fist.

ERRATA

p.3.1.7. for 'himself' read 'his shelf'

p.7.1.3. for 'his shelf' read 'himself'

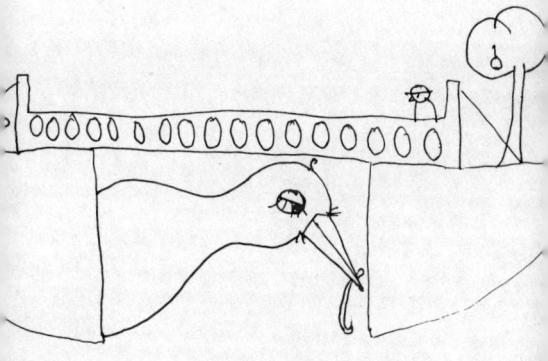

HARD CROUCHER

A hen, sitting by a fence, crouches
hard against the wood.

FLY SANDWICH

A fly crouching in a sandwich can
not comprehend why it has become
more than ordinarily vulnerable.

BAKER

I was cutting The Earth, when snow
fell and made an extra layer.

MOTH MOVE

I see the moth move but I do not
know what it is doing.

IN NORWAY

Gentlemen and ladies in bed whispering misunderstanding — as though whispering in English.

BELL BREAKS

When the bell breaks, silence sweeps
across the moor. If you lie in a hollow
you will not escape.

PATH HERE

There is not a path here. I can not
meet you. I see you across the grass.
We smile and wave hands.

GOOD TELECOMMUNICATIONS

Thanks to good telecommunications
we know much more about the *amount*
of suffering going on in the world.

SOME SUBSTANCE

The housefly pauses to wipe some substance from its legs and simultaneously ease an intolerable itch.

RED BUTTON

A button on my shoe. A red button
on a black shoe. The wool stocking
hides the ankle so the button shows
off.

SPOUSE

One day you are no longer interesting.

GREEDY MISER

A greedy miser, fallen in love, wrote a card in whole letters to proclaim her generosity. The object of her affections, who was no fool, and a graphologist to boot, observed the whole letters with amused disdain, and replied, accusing her of being a greedy miser. He was a greedy miser himself, and knew whole letters as an old false generosity trick used by greedy misers when writing love letters.

TEN YEARS

I spent ten years at the conservatoire learning how to listen. After graduating with an A+, I gave several concerts, sitting on a chair listening to restive audiences. Eventually they started bringing instruments and went home after, thrilled with the quality of my reception.

NATURE

Men with large bellies instinctively balance themselves. Before Newton, large people crawled.

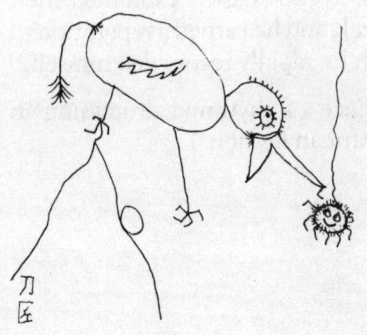

TERRIFIED KOOKABURRA

A terrified kookaburra yearned for anonymity, but was unable to repress his maniacal natural laugh. He flew to a mountain top, like a film star, and shouted himself hoarse, but his laugh was so obscene that indignant ladies in the avenue hastily examined their apparel, and he earned a reputation to which he rapidly reconciled himself.

(A piece of rhythmic drumming in the African fashion.)

THE NATURAL HEIGHT OF CLOUD

The natural height of cloud is a distance neither too high nor too low. I played a film of rain backwards and noticed that it returned to cloud at a natural height, thus affirming my contention. I then played a film of smoke backwards. Characteristically, it vanished down the chimney.

A REMOTE PORT

A remote port harbours a lost ship. The sails are washed at the launderette, piece by piece. The wood is scraped with a yellow knife. Dull stores are shipped. Inland transport is poor and costly, passing over a shiny mountain and a snowy desert. Lacklustre conferences are held in the big cabin following double-edged telephone-calls to the Oslo owners. The men are snugly bunked by lonely seawidows who have put something by at the post office. The captain becomes a teacher's assistant at a school for ragged children. He uses letters from his wife with news of home as a reading aid. To keep busy, he hollows a cave out of a great sandstone boulder alone in a field. Years pass, but, without natural resources, the town does not change. The captain sails the ship into the open sea, but she sinks beyond the point and he swims to a village two or three miles up the coast where he remains, digging a slow hole through the shiny mountain.

I LAID DOWN THE LUMP

I laid down the lump of wood and climbed on a goose. He flew me along the sky. My head touched and our shadow showed. He looked at me, then tipped me slowly over a grey cloud. My pullover caught on a crag and saved my life, but when I reached home my lump of wood had gone. 'One lump of wood is like another lump of wood,' they said soothingly. The goose winked at me so I ate him. After tea I found my wood but could not put the goose together. I would not touch the wood till I stopped feeling bad.

AN UGLY FACE

When asked to work we look askance,
turn and walk to the window, humming petulantly through tight lips.
Holding the unfinished task, you sidle
up and wave it to and fro with an old
kind of smile, tugging our woollen
hems and disarranging the warp. Sen-
sing your increasing interest in our
legs etc, we move to the table in a
stiff way, straightening our shoulders
and sucking in our chests, picking
our teeth with our tongues to make
an ugly face. Pleased but frustrated
you return to your glass office in the
corner and pretend to make a local
call into the telephone, legs crossed,
admiring your shoe.

SEE ME

"See me!" screamed the old woman and tottered off the cliff. The sharp wind up her coat revived her interest in life for a few bitter-sweet seconds.

FOR A LARK

One night, for a lark, we inverted all the trees in the park. It was spring, and we could hear the fledglings chirping 20 feet below the earth, delighted to be close to their food supply. The park keeper nearly had a fit, but he was both a fatalist and an ecologist so he just changed the name of the park and took notes. That year, the sparrows grew to the size of small ostriches.

HAIR CRACK

An old man points to a hair crack on his teacup with a withered nail. His niece smiles, admires his eyesight and, for the first time, really looks at his eyes. They are not clear, but bleary. 'Those black dots is where the picture goes in, the hair crack registers.'

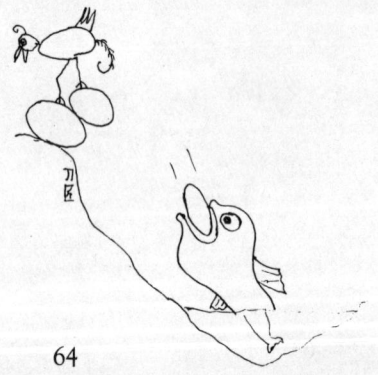

KEVIN'S CLUMSY TOUCH

'Do not smile when you lie,' Mrs L. ineffectually begged her daughter, 16 the day before. Linda smiled, feeling cool in her cotton print, running her red nails down its factory freshness, aching for Kevin's clumsy touch and a glass of lager and lime in her hand; the juke box on its rubberised supports.

THIN GRUEL

Ladies like to be cool. Their feet lie in streams. Fresh fish investigate the flavour with a wise frown. Young women chew gum as they chat about men. The thin gruel of their thoughts is not heard at a distance. I walk quietly by, a paracetamol in my mouth.

QUALIFIED NURSE

I bend, head between your knees,
trying not to faint. 'I am a qualified
nurse,' she blushes and feels her purse
for a copy of her credentials, the
original in a frame on her parents'
wall, covered over with wallpaper.
'Our girl's a nurse,' they tell visitors,
the plumber, say. 'She's a fainting
specialist.' 'I'm better now,' i mutter,
removing my head regretfully, aware
of how clean you are.

A ROBIN AND A RHEA

If all birds were disposed of except a robin and a rhea it would be difficult to persuade even the gullible that they were kin. The robin would give you the horse laugh. 'I'm an insect,' he would jeer. Likewise the rhea would find links with the kangaroo who is not a bird at all though seeming to try to take off constantly.

A BROWN SHAPE

A crowd walked round the barrier. They were a unit. 'Who is your nucleus?' I quavered. They looked about them and became still. 'We are moved by the same need,' they rumbled. 'Then line up.' I called. They lined up, then the line wavered and they drifted back. I clutched a straggler. 'What happened?' 'As a line we lost our impetus.' And shambled off, a brown shape.

RHEUMATICY BUSH

A thick bush full of prickles, I stand
between the desert and the sea. Arabs
in bathing costumes avoid me, mutter-
ing from right to left, as is their way.
My bright eyes peer at the sea, smile
at the sailcloth bellying from a mast.
Salty sand and sandy salt is my diet.
So many crystals, my swollen joints
fear the rain.

DEMON

A demon stepped into a puddle by a children's boating loch. Coughing furiously, he climbed into a rowing boat and rowed round and round, his bony knees up by his ears in the darkness. After, he smoked a cigarette on the jetty, still coughing.

TROUBLE

When I felt her legs and discovered that there were two, I knew that there was going to be trouble.

BANANA SANDWICH

She left the room. A shawl lay across
the chair. It was warm and smelled of
lavender. I sat and looked at the door,
because it would open and I would
walk along the corridor to the stairs.
It was dark and I did not move, except
to put on the red shawl and eat a
banana sandwich from my holdall.
How still the air is in the room! I am
ashamed to breathe, sucking in mov-
ing air. But nobody counts air nor
grudges a few mouthfuls. She returns
and pulls on her shawl. I follow as far
as the stairs. 'No farther,' she says
and departs. I burn an envelope to
keep warm. Made bold by impatience
I remove the stairrods and await her
return, grinning in the dark.

TUCK IN

An ant and a bee sit to eat. It is a
spider. 'I am afraid to die,' he moans
as they crunch off his legs. There is a
respite to break wind, then they boot
him across the field to bruise his tis-
sues. 'Do not be afraid,' they sing as
they tuck in, 'And look at the sky.'
But he is.

RENAISSANCE

There is to be a renaissance. Poetry and painting, smiles and home-made dresses. Even ploughmen will fart louder to scare gulls off useful worms.

PARALLELEPIPED

The old couple built a house of Welsh stone but it was badly pitched and came to a slant like a parallelepiped. Architects came in the evenings in cars and stood around stealing the idea. Slates split with the strain.

FEELING THE NEED

Feeling the need for company I sought
out a large group of people and stood
among them walking and turning
smiling and frowning then returned
home.

ON THE DAY

On the day that cars were banned
motorists sat on the road in chairs
protesting each with a china plate
held between his hands.

BIG BLUE LID

Rolled beef boils under a big blue lid.
We tuck feet under the wooden table
and wait. Mother hums a light tune
and smiles. Her head lights up. 'Look
at the beef!' we beg Father who entered
by the door. Toes curl and mouths run
as his hand presses firmly on the meat,
then uses the knife.

FISH PROFESSOR

Having spent eight years trying to teach his pet herring to cough, but without success, a perverse ichthyologist went out and bought a lungfish and a box of Havanas.

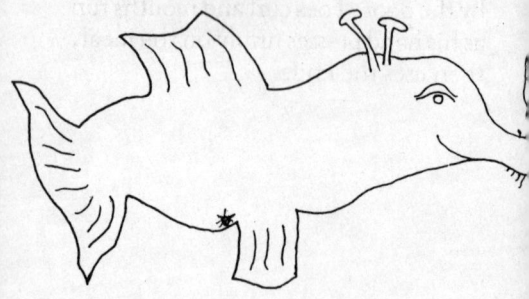

GAOLBIRDS

An elephant and a hippopotamus discover themselves lying in adjacent
cells. They spend the night discussing
old days in the jungle in frantic whis-
pers, not once mentioning their reasons
for being jailbirds.

DISAPPOINTED

The sun disappointed me so I crawled
under the ground. There was neither
night nor day. I did not know when
to sleep. My sandwiches ran out. The
temperature was even. I could not be
alone — an animal was always burst-
ing in and with a muttered apology
was gone. The same with insects. Yet
the cool earth was to my taste and up
above like madmen life went on. Only
once did I return, for some underwear.

SMELL MY BREATH

Every girl thrills in our village —
Wayne is back! Hello, Wayne. See
my pretty button nose, my hair, short
and cheeky. My matching hat, gloves,
hankie and handbag — and my lovely
shape. Smell me, Wayne — and smell
my breath. I'm yours Wayne. Ring
me at home.

HEEL MARK

A man walks on the prairie. He does not move — there is no mark to measure his progress. In despair, he digs a hole with his heel, leaves it, and before a week reaches the far edge. 'I dug a hole,' he tells his friend, swallowing beer.

TOUCHSTONE

Please mister, will you be my touchstone? Sitting by you sets me straight. Thank you. Please lady will you be my touchstone?

Go away or I'll call the police. Touchstone! Whatever next! I saw you with that man. You sat by him. Touchstone! Sitting by a man!

INCONSEQUENCE

A sailor caught my eye as I stood exposed, comfortably emptying my bladder, nodded toward the venereal infection notice and winked. I smiled faintly, embarrassedly unable to match his air of inconsequence.

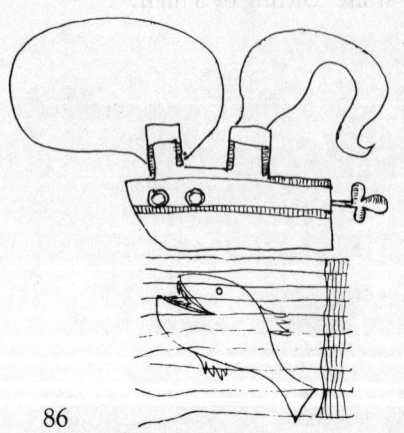

BUFFET

A lady found an insect on her body.
Fainting with dusgust and observing
she was alone she fetched it a slap.
Shocked by the buffet it limped off to
die in a dark place between her
shoulder-blades out of reach. There
was quite a little community there,
mostly daddy-long-legs and moths,
either crippled or convalescent. 'Talk
about using a steamhammer to crack
a nut,' they mumbled or buzzed,
incensed by her rough and ready
behaviour.

LUNATIC

Living creatures, completely unaware of Man's immortal soul see him only as a vicious destructive creature with an infinite capacity for making a mess, unable to relate to The Earth and without aesthetics. As a dying butterfly was heard to whisper:—

"He's a fucking lunatic!"

SCRABBLY HARD TOUCH

A cock's claws are not fashioned for intimacy, for tenderness. Does the cock know this? Does it, quietly in the hen house, caress the hen's breast? In the semi-light, the old hen in the corner, eyes rheumy from the sting of droppings, trying hard to remember a claw's light hard scrabbly touch. A moment of hot delight illuminates her and she leans back in the dark with a soft cluck.

MELON

A big man swung an axe into a melon.
Where's my axe? he mumbled and
went home. A family found the yellow
beauty and ate it for dessert after their
egg and tomato sandwiches. The axe
was tossed casually aside. They had
never eaten a melon and thought it
was the bone. One day at school, the
child was asked where do axes come
from? Melons he could have said but
did not know its name so he held his
peace. He did not know axe either.

LARGE AND YELLOW

The cliff was so high that when you stood at the top you looked down at the sun. A strong girl rowed a boat to the horizon where the sun was. The sun obligingly waited for she was pretty. How large and yellow you are, she said, walking over it on her bare feet, for she did not want to burn her new plimsoles. No one would believe her, so she took a photo, but it did not come out.

AN INFORMED TASTE

An intelligent bull owned by an irascible farmer asked by a wag whether he preferred Seurat to Jackson Pollock bellowed I can't for the life of me see the difference. Stuck out here I don't get a chance to go round the galleries and develop an informed taste. The wag shamed bought him a small Morland.

A SUCCESSFUL INTERIOR DESIGNER

A tractor of the type used for pushing combine harvesters farther up the field ran over a palomino with a highwayman on it busy chasing a stranger who consequently never knew that he'd been chased. The highwayman was a successful interior designer who loved adventure for its own sake.

O QUARTZ!

Sand is blowing. i.e. stones are blowing. A minute insect cries — stones are blowing! — or boulders even. So if a grain of sand hits you it's like being hit by a house. Sandflies are the bravest creatures on the world. They pray to the wind god to let up and their worst oath is — O quartz!

HOW DO YOU DO

A man was thirsty. He ran after a camel. The camel stopped till he caught up. The man did not know what to do.

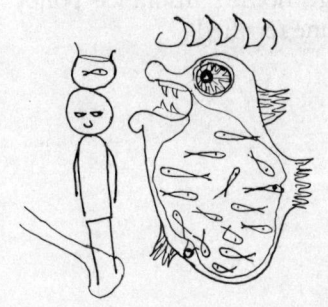

DOGGED PERSISTENCE

A man looked out the window every night at 6 to watch the sun set. A large house blocked the way and the sun never set at 6 but that did not deter him. Proud and independent many people admired his dogged persistence for he was not frivolous. His neighbours were unable to renew their large house's insurance policy and became terrified.

DIRTY SKY

Imperfection is an integral part of per-
fection. Oh! You ventrally-squashed
toothpaste tube! Oh! You dishes in
the sink and hair in the plughole
mingled in gray fat! Oh! You healthy
fear! Oh! You clerks that trust comp-
uters and smell of chips. Oh! You cities
built on top of the ground! Oh! You
dirty sky that I can't see the stars and
acid in the rain! Oh! You dirty sky!
Oh! You dirty torn sky!

FRUSTRATION

The dog stood in the mud unable to move flashing its teeth. The angry man with the torn trousers stepped briskly away humming tightly. The amused young woman in her see-through baby-doll touched by the dog's frustration threw her cat out the window on to the mud beside it switched on her favourite mindless rubbish and lifted her nail-varnish from the padded dressing table.

HER DARLING

Even as a child cloth was magic. Her
mum who massaged in the sauna shop
brought books of patterns home from
the tailor next door. She lay on the
linoleum on her stomach soaking in
texture with her good eye while Mum
boiled a soup cube pulled a white roll
open and poured in sandwich spread
for her darling.

A WARP AND A WOOF

She has a body covered with skin —
and there is cloth, which is a woman's
madness — a warp and a woof. The
idea of placing cloth on her skin
makes her mad with excitement. She
compares the cloth's texture with her
skin and gasps. When she covers her
body with a dress she waits for things
to happen. Basically, that a man will
take it back off.

TINY TWISTS OF THE WRIST

A blue thin coat-belt lying flat over my wrist taken for a walk. It must not fall. Balanced, tiny twists of the wrist hold its equilibrium as I move along the grass. It is a game taken seriously not easy to explain to a passer-by. Foolishly, I hold my breath bend my knees twist my wrist in vain. Later washing the dishes I successfully float a saucer.

BELLY

The only belly which uses wind constructively is the belly of a sail. Because of social embarrassment no one has tried to put our own personal wind to use propulsive or otherwise.

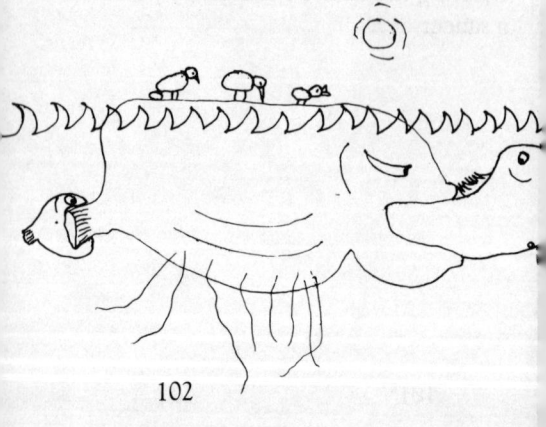

JAMBOREE

At a girl guide jamboree it was possible with sensitive equipment to record the sound of acne developing. Played to boy scouts they got excited when told what it was. Many started to masturbate, but were given wholesome advice by uneasy scoutmasters.

MALICE

Out of malice, I bored a hole through a bucket then set the house on fire. We were soaked as it passed up the chain and it was empty at the crucial spot but we needed every bucket so it kept circulating.

At the post mortem everybody affirmed independently how it had kept them amuzed. Leaky buckets were a fashion for umpteen years.

POLISH THE BELL

Polish the bell no scour the bell hey boys listen that's a 32 gauge bell what a faint delicate ding must have scoured the clapper ding

oh boy that's a delicate bell I could listen till Tuesday I mean Thursday I forgot today's Tuesday should have known it's Einstein's birthday.

NAKED

Naked, she held the moon in a towel.
It was larger than it looked in the sky.
Its rays glowed on her skin. 'My mother
says it will make me irresistible.' I
watched as she returned it to the sky.
Like the London moon she was not
too bright. How about the sun? I asked
when she came down.

BIRD RAIN

Birds rained into the water, gulped at nervously by shining grey fish. Vacuums appeared in the air so they fell. Fierce birds, eagles and falcons as well. Dodos and moas toppled in. Herring did particularly well but flounders got their share. I'll never forget the surprize on an ostrich's beak.

EG

A hen blinks at an eg, the most beaut-
iful sight in the world. I wish I could
lay you again and again, she clucks,
gloating, forgetting yesterday's eg and
the day before's. her feathers squeeze
and twist against the wire cage, claws
warm with drippings.

A CRAFTY BURGLAR

Black frost nibbles a fence of rotting sleepers in smoking darkness. High over the hill a blue curly moon dances, motionless. A jolly youth feels the axe-haft in his hand as he steps to the wood. 8 quick blows sever a tree. sap spills about the grass — stickies his boots. Hearing the dawn, he departs. His wide eyes suck the light. The boring dawn — the paling moon — the cry of a hen in pain. The red sun, a crafty burglar, pounces on the spaces between the tips of the grass, then rushes over the landscape like a wound, to lie in the valley.

AN UNHAPPY MEDIUM

The excitement of a poet is his vision, and the words. These are not the man himself. Those who talk with a poet are bewildered by his ordinariness and the poet is hurt by their reaction, because he too thought he was more than he is.

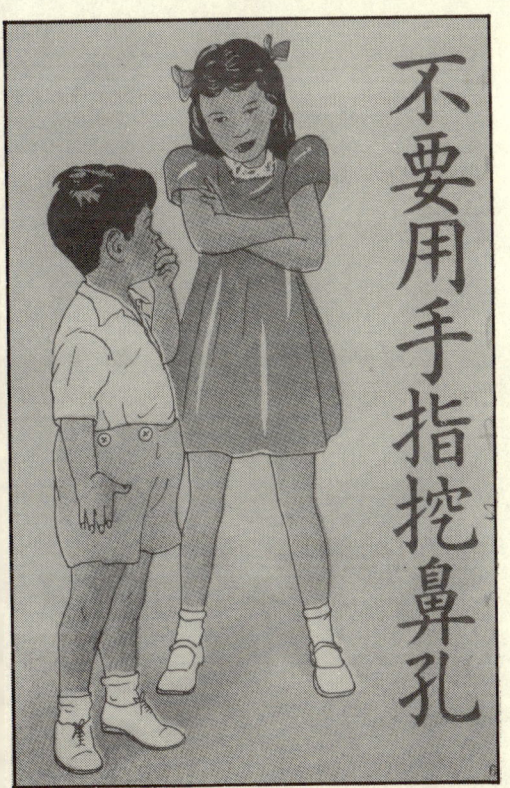

不要用手指挖鼻孔